CONTENTS

▶ IN CLASS

Scan this page to download all the audios and videos you need in this module.

▶ OUT OF CLASS

OUR FOCUS THIS WEEK:

Finding out about activities and places, and planning a great weekend.

BUILDING THE PROJECT

STAGE 1 — Getting started

STAGE 2 — How's it going?

STAGE 3 — Working together

STAGE 4 — Putting it together

STAGE 5 — Sharing what you did

DAY 1

BEFORE YOU BEGIN....

Find out three things about your classmates.

1 DIVING INTO ACTIVITIES

Look at the photos. What kind of activities can you see?

2 CLOSE UP

Look at the photos again.

- Which activities have you tried?
- Why? Why not?
- What's your opinion about them?

Yes
↓
Why?
↓
What was it like?

No
↓
Why not?

Would you like to?
Why?   Why not?

Make a note here.

Done ….

I would like to do these …

I wouldn't like to do these …

REASONS WHY

Compare your opinions with your classmates.
Tell them about other activities you like.

4 CLASS CHECK

Which activities are
- most popular?
- least popular?
- the most unusual?

5 BEST WEEKEND EVER

Here are some blog posts about weekend activities.

Match the different blog posts with the pictures.

A

The best weekends? In the spring and summer!

I go hiking.

I get up really early. I usually grab some food from the kitchen (Mum's not always happy about this!).

I meet my mates at the bus-stop. One of them's always late and misses the bus. Stupid!

The roads are usually pretty empty – sometimes I just go to sleep again. But I love watching the sunrise – awesome!

When the bus stops, we get out and start walking. I like being in the hills. It can be scary if the clouds are low. But the views are fantastic on a good day!

We tell stories and sing – and stop for lunch in one of our favourite places.

Oh – and we record the miles we walk – so it's a kind of competition.

I'm often the winner!

Karen 15

B

My sister and I love surfing! We're not very good – but we're learning quickly. Oh – Dad thinks we're brilliant, of course!

We go to the beach by campervan with Mum and Dad. They like looking at plants and insects, and taking photos. Millions of them. Honestly, it's pretty cool!

The beach is often empty, and the waves are huge – it's really exciting. But some days the wind's too strong – so surfing isn't safe. We go and sit in a café and watch other people (people-watching!). Boring.

Anyway, surfing's a great sport. It makes you strong... and it's fun. Better than doing homework at the weekend.

Petra 14

C

I like working at weekends. Yeah, really! It's great!

My aunt's cool. She has a stall in the local market – selling jam and honey. It's from her farm - it tastes fantastic. People love it – so I'm really busy. They chat – and taste things, too.

There's a real 'buzz' at the market – I love listening to the noise and watching people. It's my home town, so I know a lot of the people, apart from the tourists.

They often have some very strange questions! But I try to help them.

Well – in the afternoon, I help my aunt with the clearing up (and counting the cash!).

In the evening, I relax – I love singing. I'm part of a choir group – we sing rock and pop. Then we just hang out ... gotta love the weekends!

Chris 17

Find the different words for 'very good' in the posts.

(Abc) Write them in the WORD-BUILDING BOX to use later.

WORD-BUILDING: POSITIVE OPINIONS

6 TALKING ABOUT IT

Discuss these questions about weekend activities.

- Which weekend activity is most similar to yours?
- What do you do to get away from schoolwork at the weekend?
- Which is the most unusual weekend – and why?
- Who has the most fun?
- Which activity could you do near here?
- Which one could you do at home?
- Which ones would be OK in the winter?
- Which activity sounds best? Why?

USEFUL LANGUAGE

- In my case,
- To be honest,
- I've got to say ...
- ... could be cool / awesome / boring / hard work
- I love .... I'm not into ...
- Too cold / wet / hard / ...
- Do you know anyone who does any of these things?

7 RECAP

Look at the comments on weekend activities in the blog posts again. Find these phrases.

We start walking.   I love surfing.   They like looking at insects.

clearing up   counting the cash   people-watching

LANGUAGE CLOSE-UP: PERSONAL OPINIONS

I LOVE ...!

Notice that in English we often use the *–ing* form to describe activities.

Singing is great!   Surfing makes you strong.   I love working in the market.

It works like a noun.

It is useful when we want to express our personal opinions in phrases such as:

I like ...   I hate ...   I don't mind ...

Look at the blog posts on page 3 again and circle all the *–ing* words you can find.

You can write some of your own examples here:

I like _____.   I love _____.

I don't mind _____.   I hate _____.

_____ is great!   _____ is okay.

_____ is awful!

8 HERE AND AT HOME

Talk about yourself and your weekend activities at home.
- Compare your weekend activities at home.
- Which are the most / least popular in your class?
- Which ones can you do here?
- What new weekend activities do you want to try?

I love ...

At weekends, I often go to ... because I like ...

I don't mind ...

But I really hate ... It's ...!

Make a weekend activities chart for your class (1=low, 10=high).

AT HOME	HERE
10	
9	
8	
7	
6	
5	
4	
3	
2	
1	
0	

(P)

What affects people's choices?
- The cost?
- The weather?
- The time?
- Their personal likes and dislikes?

9 PLANNING ACTIVITIES: WEATHER FORECAST

What's the weather like at home now? Check your weather app.

- What about here? And tomorrow? The rest of the week?
- How much weather information can you find?
- Will this weather affect your weekend activities? How? Why?

10 LANGUAGE CLOSE-UP: DESCRIBING THE WEATHER

(Abc) **What weather words do you know?**

Put them in this table.

	sun	rain	wind	hot	cold	other
Light						
Medium						
Extreme						

Check out these extra weather words and phrases.

showers   sunny spells   drizzle   stormy   freezing   chilly   damp   overcast   misty
cloudy   warm   pouring   boiling   It's quite nice out.   It's howling a gale.

Decide where to put them in the table.

Which ones can describe the weather here today? Or at home?

11 LOCAL WEATHER

(•)) **Listen to three people talking about their local weather.**

Write a, b or c to link the conversations and the pictures.

LISTEN UP!

Notice where and when you hear phrases like this outside the classroom. Note them in your journal.

(•)) **Listen again and complete these statements.**

It's a bit _____ /_____ /_____ today!

_____ /_____ /_____ outside, isn't it?

It's really _____ / It's really _____ in the sun.

/ It's really _____ today.

Listen to your teacher's instructions for a role play.

> Make the forecast for this week.
> Compare with other people. Are they optimistic or pessimistic?
> What do local people think?
> Will it affect your weekend activities?
>
> **Write your forecast in your journal. Check it each day – were you correct?**

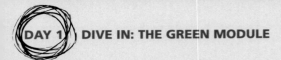

12 ACTIVITIES AND FEELINGS

Check back through pages 2-5. Note any new language.

- What are you doing this week that is unusual?
- Why is it unusual? What do you feel about it?
- Compare with your classmates.

13 TALKING ABOUT EXPERIENCES

What about the people in this photo?

- What are they doing? How are they feeling?
- Discuss your ideas with your classmates.

What questions do they ask? What are their answers? Write their conversation.

Practise your conversation, then perform it for the class.

14 GETTING TO KNOW YOUR CLASSMATES

What can you find out about two classmates? Prepare some questions to ask them.

Then make notes here. ☞

	Name 1	Name 2
Likes doing …		
… because…		
Not so keen on …		
… because ….		
Is planning to do ……		
at the weekend.		
Other plans?		

Don't forget your Journal.

🖐 **See if you can make a note of three things from today.**

THE DAY 1 TO DAY 2 BRIDGE

1 Look back at page 2.
What photos would you choose for activities here?

2 What new activities do you want to try here?
Which ones are similar to home? Which ones are different?

3 CHECK IT AND USE IT
What new ways have you discovered for talking about the weather?

5 What have you discovered about your classmates? Any surprises?

LANGUAGE LINKS

Take a look at LANGUAGE WORKOUT 1 on page 34. Describing activities.

Don't forget LANGUAGE SUPPORT on pages 46-53.

Don't forget to record your ideas in your journal.

THE PROJECT ☞ STAGE 1 Getting started

Let's get started today on our new project ...
'Finding out about activities and places, and having a great weekend'.

BEFORE WE BEGIN

Our project will help us explore the place where we are staying, meet the people who live here and discover the things that are different from home.

We can then decide how to describe this place to our classmates and to people at home.

ORGANISING AND PLANNING

Discuss these things with your group.

- Who will be in our group?
- What information do we want to include?
- Where can we find the information?
- How will we present our project? A video? A live presentation?
- Who will do what?

USEFUL LANGUAGE

What about doing a .....?
Or how about a .....?
I'd rather do a .....
We could do a .....
We need to get on with it!

You'll need a small notebook to use as a Project Diary. Keep your notes there.

DAY 2

1 DIVING INTO PLACES

Look at the photos. What kind of places can you see?

2 CLOSE UP

Look at the photos again. Match these descriptions with the places.

rocky coastline   cliffs   fields   beach   lane   moor
lake   hills   river   track   cycle path   farmland

Add some more words to describe the places.

SAY IT BETTER

🔊 Listen and practise the pronunciation.

Where would you most / least like to go? Why?

3 HERE AND AT HOME

Talk to other people in your class.

* Do you have similar places at home? Compare with other people.
* Which places are most common? Which ones are most unusual?
* Which places can you see near here?
* Which ones do you want to visit? Why? Compare your ideas.

4 WHERE TO DO THINGS

Look at the photos again. Think about cities, too.
What outdoor activities can people do in each place?
Make a note here.

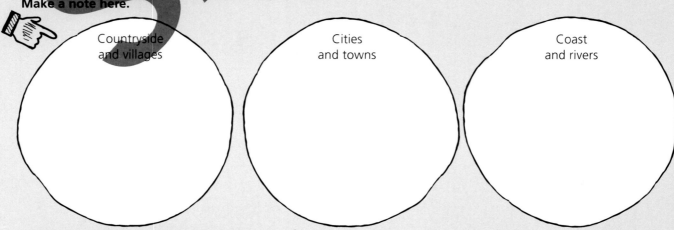

Countryside and villages

Cities and towns

Coast and rivers

Compare your ideas and add extra ones.
Look back at the activities in Day 1. Which places are good for those activities?

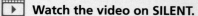

5 VIDEO TIME: GUESS WHAT'S HAPPENING!

Look at the places photos on page 8 again and check their names.

You are going to watch five conversations in five different places.

- Where do you think each conversation takes place?
- What do you think the conversations have in common?

6 PREDICTING AND CHECKING

 Watch the video on SILENT.

- Were you correct about the places?
- Predict five phrases you expect to hear. Add them to the bingo card.

Now watch the video WITH SOUND.

Were you correct about the phrases?

7 YOUR TURN!

Choose one of the situations from the video cartoon sequence.

- **Find a partner and recreate the conversation.**
- **If necessary, create your own cue cards.**
- **Perform your conversation and listen to the others.**
- **Comment on them.**

LISTEN UP!

How often do you hear these phrases this week? Where?

EXTENDING

If you have time, change your partner, and the landscape.

Create a new conversation.

8 LANGUAGE CLOSE-UP: IDENTIFYING PLACES

(Abc) COMPOUND NOUNS

Look at these words. Which of the places can you match to activities in this module?

beach hut   bike shop   bowling alley   tennis club   riverbank   seaside   shopping mall   town centre

These names of places are made by putting a noun and a noun, or an *-ing* and a noun together.

Put these examples in the correct box.

noun + noun

REMEMBER!

With a compound noun, the second word is the place, person or object you are talking about. The first word describes it. So:

mountain bike = a bike for the mountains

bike shop = a shop that sells bikes

Some compound nouns are written as one word (*seaside, hilltop*), while others are two words (*beach hut, tennis club*).

-ing + noun

Can you think of any other compound nouns? Write them in the correct box.

9 WORD RACE

What are these compound nouns? Identify them with a partner.

the house on a farm   _____

the top of a mountain   _____

a special village for holidays   _____

a town beside the sea   _____

a restaurant that sells sushi   _____

a market that sells antiques   _____

Which pair can finish first?

Write four similar puzzle questions for other pairs to solve.

_____

_____

_____

_____

CLASS CHECK

Combine all your compound nouns to make a reference list.

10 FINDING OUT ABOUT PLACES

Look at the photos of places on page 8 again.

With your partner, think of questions to ask about them.

> Is it always cold?
>
> Where is it?
>
> What's it called?
>
> Do people live there?

11 LANGUAGE CLOSE-UP: REGISTER

STRANGERS AND FRIENDS

Can you spot the difference?

Look at these requests and decide if they are polite (P), informal (I) or neutral (N).

_____ Can I just ask whether there's a lake near here?

_____ Sorry, is there a lake near here?

_____ Could you tell me if there's a lake near here?

_____ I wonder if you could help me. Is there a lake near here?

_____ I fancy going swimming. Is there a lake near here?

Listen to the requests for information.
- What do you expect the answers to be?
- Compare your ideas.
- Listen to the conversations and check.

LISTEN UP!

How often do you hear these phrases this week? Where?

12 CHATTING ABOUT PLACES

Here is part of an instant message exchange between two friends.

Complete the responses.

Hi Poppy!

Where _____?

I'm in the country.

Wow! What's _____?

Fantastic! It's really green.

Sounds good.
Where _____?

In a big house. Near a lake.

Lucky you!
What _____?

Well, there are boats to hire. And jet skis – but I'm too scared!

And the weekend?
What _____?

Guess!

No idea. Tell me!

We're going up in a hot-air balloon! Over the hills and perhaps to the coast.

That's incredible!
I'm so _____!

I'll take some photos, for sure.

Now create a similar chat with your partner about a place here.

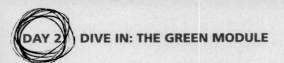
13 **FACTFILE: INFORMATION FOR VISITORS**

Here is a map with some typical Tourist Office information for visitors.

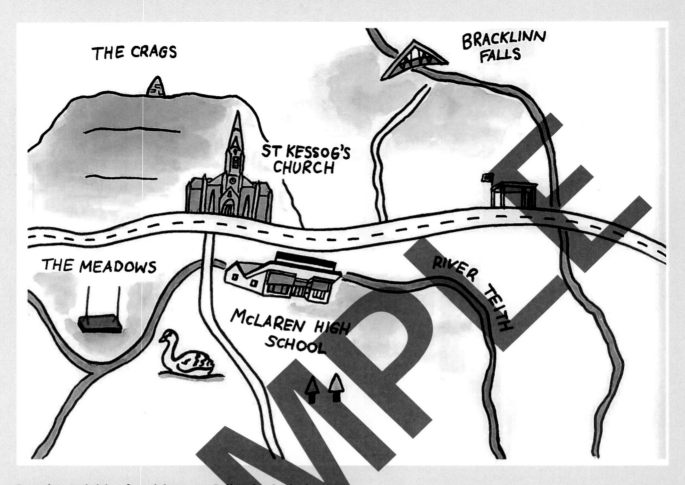

Popular activities for visitors to Callander include:

- hiking on the paths to the north of town
- canoeing on the river
- watching wildlife
- visiting historic buildings, like St Kessog's church
- taking photos of the waterfalls
- … and much more!

But, there's a problem: the activities are missing from the map! Descide where to put them and complete the map. Add some more weekend activities to do here. Writes these new ideas here:

14 **FINDING OUT ABOUT THIS AREA**

Ⓟ Is there a similar Tourist Office map on the Internet for where you are staying?

- Check out the information.
- Is it interesting? Is it easy to understand?
- What facts and information can you add?
- Compare your ideas.

THE DAY 2 TO DAY 3 BRIDGE

What do you think about these things?

1 Look back at the photos of places from today.
Which ones do you like best? Why?

2 Remember the conversations on the cartoon video?
Choose a different situation. Think of 2 crazy characters.
Create a conversation and make it funny.

3 CHECK IT AND USE IT
Look at page 11 again.
Did you learn anything new about using polite, informal or neutral language? Record some examples on your phone.

4 What information is important for visitors to this place?

5 What have you discovered about your classmates today?

LANGUAGE LINKS

Take a look at LANGUAGE WORKOUT 2 on page 35.
Explaining where things are.

Don't forget LANGUAGE SUPPORT on pages 46-53.

Don't forget to add important things to your journal.

THE PROJECT ☞ STAGE 2 How's it going?

Now let's carry on with our project ...
'Finding out about activities and places, and having a great weekend'.

CHECKING THINGS TODAY

Check your Project Diary. Compare your notes with the rest of the group.

Discuss your progress from yesterday. Agree what needs to be done next.

Who's doing what?

How much time do we have?

Are there any problems? Who can help?

Do you want to change anything?

What have you discovered about local places and activities here?

USEFUL LANGUAGE

How about being an editor? You're good at it!

I'm going to ...

How about you?

Decide these things before you go on to Stage 3.
Make notes in your Project Diary.

DAY 3

1 DIVING INTO INDOOR ACTIVITIES

Look at the photos. What kind of activities can you see?

2 CLOSE UP

Look at the photos again.

- Which activities have you tried?
- What's your opinion about them? Positive or negative?

> *I think bowling is really boring!*

> *No! I don't agree. It's fun!*

Write 5 questions about favourite activities in bad weather.

Ask three classmates.

Do you like .....?

Do you ever .....?

What sort of ..... do you like ..... when ...?

What .....?

Where .....?

3 CLASS CHECK

Which indoor activities at home are ...

- most popular?
- least popular?
- the most unusual?

Which are the most popular 'rainy day' places at home? Why?

Which indoor activities can / can't you do here? Why / Why not?

4 WHAT'S THE WEATHER FORECAST?

Ⓟ Find out what the weather is going to be like for the next few days. Good? Bad?

Will it affect any activities you have planned?

5 PERSONAL FAVOURITES

Here are four blog posts about
rainy day activities. Choose one.
Read it quickly and guess the activity.

A

When the weather's bad, I love doing this – but I'm not very good at it! Well – I'm not bad – not total rubbish! But I tend to use different colours. Look – in the photo, the landscape's grey. With lots of greens. But when I use grey, it's often too dark. So I use blue and purple a lot. I like doing this when it's raining – it's creative! And when I like one of them, I put it up on my wall. Or give it to someone. So it's useful, too!

B

On the whole, I don't stay at home when it's raining.

When we can, I come here with my friends.

Sometimes we go bowling, or go to a film, but this is my really favourite thing.

It's a real laugh, trying to get the little ball over the bridges, and through the little houses and things! But it isn't cheap – we only come here every couple of months. But it's fun …you know what? Being with your friends is the best!

C

Sometimes I play online with my friends – but I talk a lot, so Mum gets irritated.

This is quiet! I can listen to music on my headphones at the same time, so that's cool.

My gaming friends often ask me to create one for them. They give me the name and the colours they like – and that gives me ideas. I can do part of it on paper, and the rest with this software.

I really love doing it – and the results are pretty good!

D

This is the best thing when it's raining.

You see, I sometimes try to sit in the living room, on the sofa, but my brother tends to want to be there. So I just go to my room – it's like going into another world there.

When I'm doing this, I can be absolutely anybody.

I have a diary, a kind of journal – but this is better.

I don't have to talk about myself – I can just imagine things!

Change one verb in each of the paragraphs.
Find the verb to change, circle it, and write it here.

1. stick _____

2. hit _____

3. design, create _____

4. write, keep _____

Work in a group. Describe your person's activity to the others in your group. Can they guess it?

- Compare the activities. Are they interesting? Why? / Why not?
- What other words could you use to describe it?

WORD-BUILDING (P)

What other unusual activities do people do?

Find or look up 4-8 new words to describe them

Write a blog post describing an activity, but don't name it.

Can your classmates guess it?

6 RECAP

Look at the comments on indoor activities in the blog posts again.

Find these phrases.

> When the weather's bad, I …

> When we can, we …

> I tend to …

7 LANGUAGE CLOSE-UP: HABITS AND FREQUENT ACTIVITIES

 To talk about personal habits and activities that we do often, we can use:
- *when* + the Present Simple
- *when* + the Present Continuous

I like doing this *when it's raining*.
When I play computer games.
I can listen to music *when I'm doing it*.

To emphasise that something is a frequent activity, we can use:
tend to + verb

I *tend to* use different colours.
My brother *tends to* want to be there.
My mum *tends to* get irritated!

8 BAD WEATHER ACTIVITIES

Look at this mind map.

Add your own ideas.

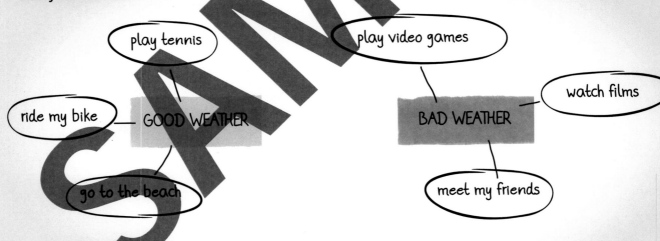

Talk about yourself and bad weather activities at home.

I tend to ….

I don't tend to ….

When I …..

When it's ….

Compare your personal bad weather activities at home with your classmates.

- Which are the most / least popular?
- Which ones are the most unusual.
- Which ones can you do here? Why? Why not?

9 PERSONAL HABITS: ONLINE ACTIVITIES

Here are some things you can do online:

- search for information
- watch videos
- play games with others
- chat to friends (speaking)

- stream live TV or films
- read articles and blog posts
- play games alone
- chat to friends (writing)

- post photos on social media
- shop online

Which ones do you do? Put them in order from most frequent (1) to least frequent (10).

Compare your activities and their frequency with other people.

> *How often do you post photos?*

> *Oh, I don't tend to do that often! I don't like doing it!*

> *Do you ever use social media?*

> *Yes, but only when I'm chatting to friends. What about you?*

Any surprises?

10 PREDICTING PERSONAL HABITS

You are going to hear some people discussing online activities.

First, look at these three extracts from the exchanges.

Circle the words you expect to hear in them.

They   they're   what are   watch   you
are they   any   just   these   water

> *.......... watching?*

> *some videos*

> *.......... good?*

> *Yes, ... not bad.*

Watson   There's a   we can   want to   do
you   what's on   this   weekend   Tessa

> *....... TV?*

> *.......a film on catch-up*

> *.......watch it?*

> *....... see what it's like.*

is   watch   less   cool   it's   Dino
I don't know   what   do you   let's

> *..... fancy doing?*

> *...... Is there anything on Netflix?*

> *....... watch 'Stranger Things'.*

> *Oh yes! The new season ....*

🔊 LISTEN AND CHECK

Were you correct? Any surprises?

11 WHAT DO YOU WATCH?

Find out what your partner watches online. Use the vocabulary in 10 and these words and phrases.

action movies   binge-watch   cartoons   comedy programmes   box sets   films
music videos   romantic films   series   series in English   videos   catch-up TV

Use *Do you like....?   Do you ever...?*   or   *What do you think of...?*

Find out more!

> *Do you ever watch black and white films?*

> *Yes, I do. I really like them!*

> *Why? What do you like?*

17

12 FACTFILE: DIFFERENT PLACES, DIFFERENT SPORTS

What do you know about popular sports here in the UK and Ireland?

- Are they indoors or outdoors?
- Talk about it with others.
- Make a class list.

- Which ones do you play at home?
- Which ones do people usually watch on TV or online?

SPORTS HERE	SPORTS AT HOME

13 UNFAMILIAR SPORTS? FACT-FINDING

Look at the photos. Do you know the sports? Choose from the following list.

GAELIC FOOTBALL, GOLF, HURLING, RUGBY, CRICKET, CROQUET, NETBALL, SHINTY, CURLING.

These are all sports which some people enjoy in Ireland, Scotland, England or Wales.

How many people do these sports in your country?

Shinty is similar to field hockey and you find it in parts of Scotland, but it isn't very famous, internationally.

Cricket is a bat-and-ball game that is popular in England, India, Australia, and other Commonwealth countries. Like rugby, many people watch it on television.

Nobody watches croquet on TV, but people play it in their gardens in summer. There's a very famous croquet match in Lewis Carroll's Alice's Adventures in Wonderland.

Netball is a popular English sport; it's like basketball, but each team has seven players on the court, not five.

Curling is a Scottish sport and you sometimes see it at the Winter Olympics, but hurling – with an H – has many fans in Ireland... but almost nowhere else.

- What can you find out about these sports online?
- Share and compare your results.
- Put your information together in a class factsheet.

14 SPORTS EXCHANGE

Are any sports in your country unfamiliar outside it?

What can you tell people about them?

15 CLASS CHECK: WATCHING OR DOING?

Decide which sports are better to watch, and which ones are better to play.

(P) Compare your opinions.

Watching sport live is best!

Why?

I don't agree. Doing sport is best!

Well, it's more exciting!

What sport do you do?

I love playing tennis.

Well, I like watching sport online.

That's lazy!

THE DAY 3 TO DAY 4 BRIDGE

What do you think about these things?

1 What have you discovered about different activities?

2 CHECK IT AND USE IT

Look at page 16 again.
How can you talk about good and bad weather activities?

3 What are some popular online activities for you and your classmates?

4 SPORTS

What did you learn about some different sports?
Any surprises?

LANGUAGE LINKS

Take a look at LANGUAGE WORKOUT 3 on page 36. Expressing frequency.

Don't forget LANGUAGE SUPPORT on pages 46-53.

Add your ideas to your journal.

THE PROJECT STAGE 3 Working together

DISCUSSING PROBLEMS AND FINDING SOLUTIONS

CHECKING THINGS TODAY

Check your Project Diary again.
Compare your notes with the rest of the group.
Discuss any problems. Try to find some solutions.
Agree what you need to do for tomorrow.

How's it going today? Are there any problems? Who can suggest some solutions?

Do you need to check out new information?

Have you met any helpful people? What have they suggested?

Do you have any new ideas about indoor activities here?

USEFUL LANGUAGE

Is everything OK?
It's going well/ OK/ slowly
I have to/ need to/ ought to + verb
This is a great photo for ...

**Discuss these things before you go on to Stage 4.
Remember: keep notes in your Project Diary.**

DAY 4

1 DIVING INTO FESTIVALS AND FUN

Look at the photos.

Can you identify any of these events in them?

air show   BBQ   carboot sale
carnival   fair   festival   fete
Highland Games   regatta   steam fair

Which events take place in these places?

village   town   city   countryside
seaside   riverside

2 CLOSE UP

- Do you have similar events in your country?
- Which events look most fun? Why?
- Compare your ideas.

3 MORE DETAILS

Match these words to the events. Some of them connect to more than one.

bric-a-brac bunting cake sale competitions costumes dancing
exhibition field food kilts knick-knacks music parade prizes
races rides second-hand stalls vintage

Check which ones are in the photos. Which words do you like best?

4 HERE AND AT HOME

Talk to other people in your class.

- Do you have similar festivals at home? Compare with your classmates.
- Which festivals are most common? Which ones are most unusual?
- What time of year do they take place?
- What happens?
- Tell the others about the festivals you like.

5 CLASS CHECK

Which festivals and activities are

- most popular?
- least popular?

20

6 **VIDEO TIME: LOCAL EVENTS**

Look at the photos on page 20 again and check their names.

You are going to watch two vloggers recommending local events.

- What do you think they are talking about?
- These numbers are in the videos. Guess their connections to the images.

£1   1st   6   11   over 30   99   500   1885   1000s

weather
neighbours

parties
smile
sport

fist bump
friends
host family

7 **WATCH CAREFULLY!**

Watch the video.

- Were you correct about the numbers?
- There are five mistakes in the video. Can you remember what they were?

Watch the video again and check.

1. _____

2. _____

3. _____

4. _____

5. _____

Choose one of the events

- What did the vloggers say about it?
- Watch the video again and check.

8 **YOUR TURN!**

Ⓟ Choose a local event.

- How would you describe it in a video?
- What numbers and details would you include?

Make factual notes here.

EVENT:

NOTES:

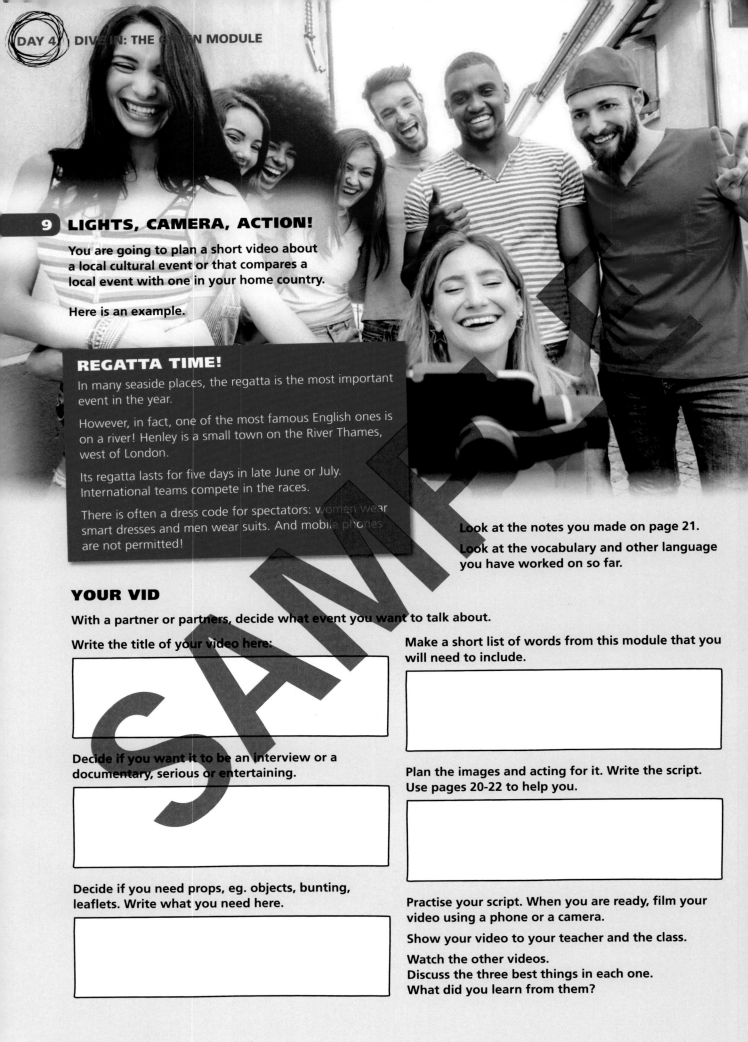

9   LIGHTS, CAMERA, ACTION!

You are going to plan a short video about a local cultural event or that compares a local event with one in your home country.

Here is an example.

REGATTA TIME!

In many seaside places, the regatta is the most important event in the year.

However, in fact, one of the most famous English ones is on a river! Henley is a small town on the River Thames, west of London.

Its regatta lasts for five days in late June or July. International teams compete in the races.

There is often a dress code for spectators: women wear smart dresses and men wear suits. And mobile phones are not permitted!

Look at the notes you made on page 21.

Look at the vocabulary and other language you have worked on so far.

YOUR VID

With a partner or partners, decide what event you want to talk about.

Write the title of your video here:

Make a short list of words from this module that you will need to include.

Decide if you want it to be an interview or a documentary, serious or entertaining.

Plan the images and acting for it. Write the script. Use pages 20-22 to help you.

Decide if you need props, eg. objects, bunting, leaflets. Write what you need here.

Practise your script. When you are ready, film your video using a phone or a camera.

Show your video to your teacher and the class.

Watch the other videos.
Discuss the three best things in each one.
What did you learn from them?

10 **LANGUAGE CLOSE–UP: DESCRIBING THINGS**

 Look back at page 10.
Check how to form compound nouns to describe places.

> **REMEMBER?**
> They use ..... + ...   or   .... form + ...

In the same way compound nouns describe **places**, you can use compound adjectives to describe **things**. Here are some useful examples.

- Circle the words that make up the compound adjective in each example.

a second-hand bookstall	a best-selling novel
handmade bunting	home-made jam
prize-winning ice cream	a world-famous regatta
old-fashioned planes	a well-known event
an indoor event	a seaside town

> **NOTICE!**
> Compound adjectives are made of more than one word. They can combine nouns, adjectives and other kinds of words in different ways. Sometimes we write them as one word (seaside), but sometimes they have a hyphen (hand-made).

Compounds are often used to describe time and distance.

a five-day regatta   a one-mile race
a fifteen-minute coffee break   a two-week course

Complete these sentences with appropriate compound adjectives.

This is a _____ lesson. It's part of a _____ course.

I want a _____ holiday when it's finished!

My route to class is a _____ walk / bus ride.

My trip here was a _____ journey!

WORD RACE

You have 6 minutes.

Write as many sentences as you can using the compound adjectives on this page.

You may not use the same adjective twice.

Your sentences must be logical and correct.

Check your partner's sentences. Are they correct? Do they make sense?

Who wrote the most sentences?

11 RESEARCHING YOUR LOCAL AREA

These phrases are missing from the signs on the noticeboard below.

What do they mean?

Look quickly at the noticeboard. Match the phrases to the signs.

Senior citizen £5.50

No drone flying!

Sold out!

Last admission 20 mins before closing

2-hour session

Refreshments available

All-weather events

Under-16s must be accompanied by an adult.

Assistance dogs

No performance Sundays

Design a noticeboard about the area where you are studying with local attractions, shows and activities.

- In a group, write short texts to go with your notices.
- Organise your group (using English). Who is doing each thing?
- Present your noticeboard to the class.

TOURIST ATTRACTIONS

Dragon Paintballing!

No minimum number of players!
Open all year.

£25 per person

Fantastic fun for birthdays or holidays.

Spend time in beautiful countryside, hide behind rocks, run through trees..... and win amazing prizes!

Come to Castell Coch!
Open summer 9.30am – 6pm

| Adults £7 |
| Under 16s £4.50 |
| Under 5s Free |

Visit the gardens! Try our home-made snacks in the tearooms

Beautiful Gothic castle originally from 13th century - a favourite with families. A castle where dreams are set!

3pm Tuesdays, Thursdays 7pm
6 days a week
Tickets: Lawn £6, Seats £8
15th – 22nd July: Romeo and Juliet
23rd – 31st July: Othello
1st – 15th August: The Tempest
Top actors bring you three fantastic Shakespeare plays.
All set in the 21st century
Fun and famous stories for you and your friends.

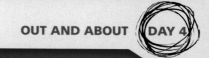

THE DAY 4 TO DAY 5 BRIDGE

More things to think about before the end of this week!

1 Look at page 20 again.
What photos would you choose for festivals?
Can you find any on your phone?

2 How many different tourist attractions can you visit here?
Take photos or record your comments on them.

3 CHECK IT AND USE IT

Look at page 23 again: describing things
Describe an interesting place here for your friends at home.

4 Any advice on finding information for tourists here?

LANGUAGE LINKS

Take a look at LANGUAGE WORKOUT 4 on page 37.
Defining and describing.

Don't forget LANGUAGE SUPPORT on pages 46-53.

**What do other people think?
How's your Journal going?**

THE PROJECT  STAGE 4 — Putting it together

THINKING AHEAD

Check your Project Diary.
Have you decided how to present your Project?
Agree what you need to do before tomorrow.

PREPARING AND PRACTISING

Here are today's check questions. You can add some of your own.

USEFUL LANGUAGE

I don't know how to...
I'm no good at ...
Can I work with you?
How about practising it later?
Have we got the ....?

When will you practise the presentation?

What will you need to present your project?

Do you need to adjust anything?

Who will do what?

**Get ready for Stage 5 tomorrow!
Update the notes in your Project Diary.**

DAY 5

1 DIVING INTO TOURISM

Look at the photos.

Name the types of tourist attractions.

2 TOURISM WORD-CHECK

What can you see or do when you visit a place as a tourist?

Make notes.

Look at a partner's list and try to memorise it. Write their words here – in 90 seconds.

Use your ideas to complete this spidergram.

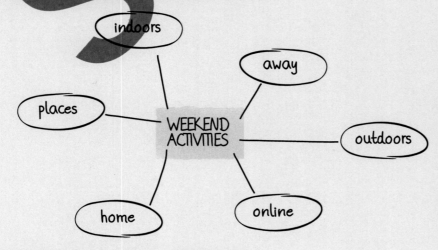

3 PLACES CHECK

Choose three of the places in the photos. Find out where they are, in the British Isles, and check out the tourist information on your phones.

Useful? Interesting? What can you add?

Were any words new for you? Which ones?

VISITING A PLACE: SOME TOURISTS' VIEWS

Some young people posted on a discussion website about tourism.
Check out their opinions.

Is tourism good or bad for our country?

LET US KNOW YOUR THOUGHTS. WE'LL GIVE A T-SHIRT TO THE 10 MOST INTERESTING ANSWERS!

VISIT US AT OUR WEBSITE

A

I like visiting seaside towns here with my parents
– but not in the summer!

You can eat fish'n'chips and cream teas. And go to the beaches.
Oh – and see the scary seagulls, and all the colours and souvenirs!

Negatives? In summer, you don't meet the people who live there,
so you don't understand what life's really like. It's very different
in winter, because a lot of things are closed. I like going in winter,
because I can meet people of my own age in a games cafe or
somewhere. I can talk to them and find out about their lives.

B

In our town, there's a well-known statue by the
sea. She's called Verity, and she was made by
a famous artist. A lot of people come to see
her. Some local people hate her – she's quite
shocking! But some of us think she's a good thing,
because the shops and hotels have lots of extra
clients now. To be honest, I love her. She's strong,
strange and beautiful. She protects us from the
sea – and from being poor.

C

We have a souvenir shop, near the river. Lots of
tourists go there, and they buy postcards and little
presents. That's great! But there's one thing I hate:
when it's raining, the tourists go to eat in cafes, but
when it's sunny, they buy stuff to eat in the street, or
by the river, or in the park. And then they just leave lots
of boxes, cups and packets everywhere. Plastic and old
food – it's horrible!

OK, tourism can be good – but what about the
environment?

Who do you agree with?

Compare your opinions.

Match these tourist tips to the posts. Then think of another tourist tip of your own.

Tidy up your litter!   Visit all year round!   Keep your eyes peeled for interesting art!

5 **CLASS TOURISM POLICY**

Choose a place you have visited as a tourist.

How could they improve it for visitors and residents?

No disposable cups or plastic straws!   *More local food!*

Work out a class tourism policy.

DAY 5

LOOKING BACK AND CHECKING

It's nearly the end of the week and of this module.
Think about the things you have discovered.

1 Look at the photos on page 26.
   What is the best tourist attraction you have found here?

2 **CHECK IT AND USE IT**
   Look at the blogs on page 27 again.
   Suggest ways in which people can be good tourists.

3 Create a keeping fit and healthy slogan for this town.

> **LANGUAGE LINKS**
> Look at your mind map in Lexical Support on pages 54-55.
>
> Don't forget to add more important words.

Share and compare your ideas and suggestions.

THE PROJECT

STAGE 5 Sharing with others

It's time to present our project ...
'Finding out about activities and places, and having a great weekend'.

FINAL CHECK
Use the notes in your Project Diary to check everything.
Check with the rest of your group.
Practise your presentation if you can.

GETTING READY, CHECKING AND PRESENTING
Points to check.

> Is the script OK? Who will check the language?

> Do we have all the photos and objects?

> Is the technology working?

> OK ... let's go!

> **USEFUL LANGUAGE**
>
> We'd like to present our ..., to you.
> We really recommend ....
> We discovered that .....
> Thanks for listening.

**Now let's see what our classmates thought of it.
And take a look at theirs.**

THE PROJECT

STAGE 5 Thinking about it all

This week, you have explored activities and places here

- in class, with your teacher and classmates.
- out of class, in your group and on your own.

You have used language, photos, and real places and people to do this.

The experience is your personal one!

EVALUATING AND DISCUSSING

How did it go?

What were the comments on it?

What have you learned from doing this project?

What have you learned from looking at the other projects?

Write your review of the project here

OUR PROJECT	
Things that worked well	Things to think about
OTHER PROJECTS	
Things that worked well	Things to think about

Was it difficult to comment on the other projects?

What's the best way to do this?

Now wrap up this week on pages 30 and 31.

WRAPPING UP: EXPLORING ACTIVITIES HERE

Here are the topics from Days 1-5:

Activities

Places and outdoor activities

Indoor activities

Festivals and fun activities

Tourism

1 PERSONAL EXPERIENCES

Look at your journal pages again as well as the pages on our day out (p. 38-39).

Do these connect to any of these topics? Which ones? How?

Which topics connect most to your classmates' week?

2 COMMUNICATING

We focussed on some key communication areas.

Expressing personal opinions   Identifying places   Discussing personal habits and activities

Describing things   Describing present and future activities   Explaining where things are

Expressing frequency   Defining and describing

Language race: your teacher will choose one area. You have 2 minutes.
Work in a team and make a list of words connected with this area.

3 EXPLORING CULTURES

Flick through the module.

Which photos give the best idea of activities here?

Suggest a word to describe them. Funny? Awesome? Strange?

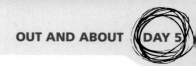 Make a note here.

PAGE	PHOTO	CULTURAL INFO	COMMENT

Look at your own photos of this place.

Which ones will you show your friends at home?

We explored different cultures: the local culture here, your own and your classmates'.

What have you learned about your classmates' cultures?

4 MODULE REVIEW

Do a review of this module to inform another class.

Use these criteria, or add your own. 5 stars = excellent!

★★★★★

CRITERIA	ACTIVITY	STARS	COMMENTS
Interest			
Information			
Discussion			
Photos			
Project			
Other			

5 USING THE EXPERIENCE

What are the things from this week's work that you will tell your friends about? Positive and negative!

THE BIG TEAM QUIZ

What can you remember?

 1 Match these words to make compounds.

side
carboot mall
home knick sale
beach hut made
knack sea
selling second crazy
hand golf best
cycle path
shopping

2 What are they called?

 Which of the words do you like best?

3 Put these sentences in the correct order.

playing we love games it's board cold when out

A. _____

_____

today warm it really is out

D. _____

_____

watch series tend I to binge Tv

B. _____

_____

countryside I really in like friends hiking the with my

E. _____

_____

boating tell if a could lake there's you here me near

C. _____

_____

and online it playing is helps fun my English

F. _____

_____

4 Circle the wrong word in each sentence. Then write a better word.

A. Making **photos** is really easy with a phone. I love doing it!

_____

B. To be **case**, I don't really like reading very much. It's pretty boring.

_____

C. It's **pouring** a gale outside, isn't it! And it's really overcast.

_____

D. I tend to watch series on catch-**in** or online, not on TV.

_____

5 How many new words beginning with C can you fit in here?

YOUR QUIZ!

Think of at least three kinds of question and write them here.

Remember: you need to know the correct answers!

DISCUSSING WHEN THINGS HAPPEN

1 THINK AND CHECK

Decide if the sentences are talking about: A. right now   B. a limited period   C. the future

1. It's freezing! Where's my scarf? ___
2. Yay! We're going surfing this weekend! ___
3. What's the man in the photo wearing? He looks strange. ___
4. The weather's boiling this summer! ___
5. I'm not eating that! It looks horrible! ___
6. Are you coming to the cinema later? ___
7. We're learning how to make honey this week. ___
8. It looks like they're having a picnic in torrential rain. _

Choose three of the sentences, one each from A, B and C. Illustrate them.

2 THINK AND WRITE

a. **Which of these sentences are true for you? Circle them.**

I'm feeling hungry.   My neighbour is talking!   I think an ambulance is passing.

This week we're doing a lot of speaking practice.   I'm making new friends.   I'm staying in a house with a garden.

We're planning our project this afternoon.   I'm going on two or three trips this week.

I'm doing something exciting later this week.

Compare which sentences you circled with a partner.

b. **Listen carefully for a moment. Look around. Write three true sentences about right now.**

_____

_____

_____

c. **Think about this week. What are you doing that is unusual for you? Write two sentences.**

_____

_____

d. **Think about later. Write two true sentences about what you're doing later today / this week.**

_____

_____

3 CREATE AND SPEAK

Read the short dialogue. What question could A ask next? Think of at least two.

What are you doing this week that you don't usually do at home?

I'm eating cereal for breakfast.

4

Find out about your classmates. Remember to ask one or two follow-up questions.

What are you doing this week that's unusual?

What are you doing later today / this week?

EXPLAINING WHERE THINGS ARE

1 THINK AND CHECK

Use these words to write captions for the photos on page 8.
Sometimes there is more than one possible caption.

on	in	near	at	by	over	towards	across

A good way to learn prepositions is to group phrases and use different colours

For example   at the beach, at the cinema, at the market, at the march, at the stables
in town, in the park, in the city centre, in the kitchen, in the river
on Park Street, on the lake, on an island, on the towpath, on the coast path

Which words can you use with *through*? *across*? *under*? *by*?

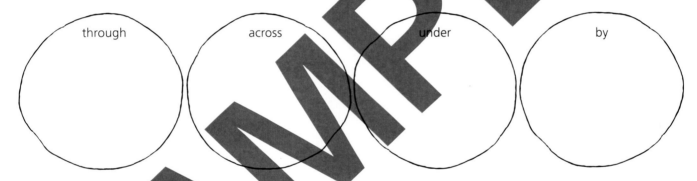

through   across   under   by

2 THINK AND WRITE

Write an email. Your teacher will give you instructions.
Write the second email here. Remember to follow your teacher's instructions.

To:

Date:

Cover your first email and
exchange with a partner.

3 CREATE AND SPEAK

Choose two photos of landscape
or places on your phone.

Describe them to your
partner to draw. Use as many
prepositions as possible.

EXPRESSING FREQUENCY

1 THINK AND CHECK

When we talk about habit, we often use the present simple with adverbs of frequency.

We often use the present simple.   *He never watches romantic films.*

It's usually warm in summer.   *I often go to the cinema on Saturdays.*   *It's generally too dark.*

There are other ways we can express frequency, too. Look at these sentences:

On the whole, I don't tend to stay at home.

We only come here **once every two months**.

Most of the time I go to my room.

Sometimes I play online with friends, but **other times** I do this.

Sometimes we go bowling or to see a film.

My Mum gets irritated **at times**.

At times, I can be a different person, too.

From time to time, friends ask me to do one for them.

Where can most of the phrases go? Circle the best option.

At the   start   end   start or end   of the sentence or clause.

Other times is the exception; it always goes after *sometimes*, and

it generally goes near the   start   end   start or end   of the sentence or clause.

Where can you put the phrases in brackets? Put a star *. You may be able to put it in two places.

I start reading a new book. (every week)   I go to a bookshop. (from time to time)

I don't read books at home. (often)   I read and write messages on my phone. (three times an hour)

I read blog posts. (hardly ever)   I doodle while I'm reading my English book. (most of the time)

I enjoy reading, and I hate it. (*sometimes…other times*)   When I feel lonely, I read. (at times)

2 THINK AND WRITE

Rewrite FOUR of the sentences in 1. Change the expression of frequency so they're true for you.

_____

_____

_____

_____

3 CREATE AND SPEAK

Find out about your classmates' reading habits. Use *How often…?* Which two classmates are most similar to you?

> *How often do you go to bookshops?*

> *I go once or twice a month. My dad works in a bookshop!*

4 Discussion. "Many 'grown-ups' say teenagers don't read. This isn't true."

Discuss in two groups. One person in each group should listen and summarise at the end.

DEFINING AND DESCRIBING

1 THINK AND CHECK

Read the example sentences.

People who go there get up very early!   *It's an ice cream which is very popular in Britain.*

Henley is a town which is on the River Thames.   *There are stalls where you can buy jam and cakes.*

There are some places where you have to wear elegant clothes.

Complete the gaps in this paragraph.

We can use *who / which* **+ verb or** *where* **+ subject + verb to give more information.**

When we want to give more information about a thing, we use 1_____, for people we use 2_____

and for places we use 3_____ with **NO** subject + verb or 4_____ **with a subject + verb.**

Match the numbers by the gaps to the example sentences above.

2 THINK AND WRITE

Solve the puzzles.

It's a place where you can buy or sell bric-a-brac in a field. _____

People who live in the same village sell cakes and organise races at this. _____

You can see tractors and usually cars which people had in the past. _____

It's an event where you can hear music, they tend to have street food too. _____

It's an adjective for things on sale which are 'not new', 'previously loved'. _____

Triangles which people put up in the street when there's an event. _____

Write three puzzles for classmates to solve.

_____

_____

_____

Read your classmates' puzzles and try to solve them.

3 CREATE AND SPEAK

Write five true sentences using the prompts.

I like people who...

_____

I love going to places where I can...

_____

I fancy trying a new hobby which...

_____

I hope I visit somewhere here where...

_____

People who ... (*hobbies*) which ...are cool / strange / fun.

_____

_____

Compare sentences. Do you agree with each other?

I think people who go ice-fishing in winter are a little crazy!

Me too! It's freezing! I prefer hobbies which are warm.

OUR TRIP OBJECTIVES

FOUR INTERESTING SIGHTS FROM THIS TRIP

FOUR UNUSUAL MEMORIES FROM THIS TRIP

THREE INTERESTING STREET OR PLACE NAMES

STORY TIME

Where? When? Who with? What did I see?

What happened? Why?

What happened as a result? How did it end?

How did I feel? How do I feel about the trip now?

Make a few quick notes here

DOODLE OF THE DAY

OUR TRIP: MORE DETAILS

PICTURE TIME

Take some close-ups for
your friends to guess.

QUIZ QUESTIONS

Write 8 questions about some of the things,
places and people from the trip.

DON'T SAY THIS!

Choose 3 objects you saw on your trip.

Find 5 words to explain each object.

Make it harder: Classmates are not allowed
to use your words in their explanation!

THE PERFECT TRIP – FOR NEXT TIME!

The best things were…

Next time, I think the trip should …

DOODLE OF THE DAY:
This sums it up for me!

 **PEOPLE**

A person I met today …

Today I was talking to …

and …

Some interesting people.

This is what I remember about them!

More thoughts about the people here.

LISTEN UP!

What's the funniest thing a person said today?

PLACES

Thoughts about the place where I'm staying.

Good things...

Strange things...

Cool things...

The best places here.

Info for my friends back home.

Places to see again.

SAMPLE

LISTEN UP!

Remember bowling alley? And beach hut? Did you hear any more interesting words for places? Make a note here.

WORDS AND PHRASES

These words stick in my mind

because …

The most useful words I've learned …

The strangest words I've learned.

SAMPLE

LISTEN UP!

Weather words - What's it like today?

(Check on page 5)

NOTICES AND SIGNS

Signs here are different from at home!
There are some photos on my phone.

Here are some of them.

Street signs

Public signs

Here in the school

My thoughts about the information in these signs.

THIS WEEK

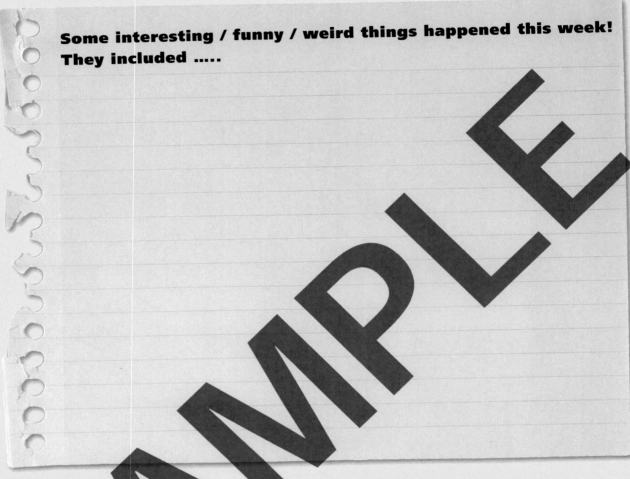

**Some interesting / funny / weird things happened this week!
They included …..**

Some of the new things I've learned this week are …..

MY JOURNAL

What do I feel about this week? Well …

_____
_____
_____
_____
_____
_____
_____
_____
_____
_____

One word to describe this week?

More thoughts about this week.

LANGUAGE BANK

The language in each module contains a variety of grammatical forms. Some of these reflect the grammatical structure of the English language. Others are functional: they help you communicate in different situations. A third group helps you with vocabulary.

You can use this Language Bank for reference and to help you remember the language you know and have practised. Add your own example sentences or translations to help you remember them.

STRUCTURAL REFERENCE

THE PRESENT TENSE: present simple and present continuous

PRESENT SIMPLE

	Use the present simple …	Your examples
London is a big city. Fresh air and exercise are good for you.	to express facts and what is generally accepted as true.	
I usually work on Saturdays. He always does his homework after dinner.	to describe habits (what *always*, *often, sometimes, never* happens).	
On Sundays I usually meet up with some friends, we go to a café, chat and play card games.	for a series of happenings (e.g. in a story).	
Nadia loves cricket.	to express attitudes / feelings.	

PRESENT CONTINUOUS

	Use the present continuous …	Your examples
I'm calling you from our hostel by the sea. The sun is shining and it's getting really hot. Dee's swimming.	to describe activities / events that are going on at the moment.	
Take an umbrella, it's raining. Why are you crying?	for temporary situations and actions that don't last long.	

THE PAST TENSE: past simple and past continuous

PAST SIMPLE

	Use the past simple …	Your examples
Australia won the Cricket World Cup in 2015. They beat New Zealand. Yesterday, I met up with my friends in a café.	for completed activities or events in the past (with *dates, yesterday, last year, a year ago* etc.).	
I made dinner, and then we watched movies all evening. Everyone went home at 2 am. It was a fun night!	for a series of actions or happenings in the past (e.g. in a story).	

PAST CONTINUOUS

	Use the past continuous …	Your examples
I was listening to music when I saw the advert for the outdoor theatre. While we were bowling, we ran into one of our teachers.	to describe the 'background' to past events, or to say what was happening when another event occurred.	
While Morgan was unpacking the picnic, Nina was taking photos.	for several activities or happenings all going on at the same time.	

LANGUAGE SUPPORT

THE PRESENT PERFECT

PRESENT PERFECT

	Use the present perfect …	Your examples
I've always liked surfing. Andy has worked in the café for six months now. I've had a lot to do since I last mailed you.	to talk about something that started in the past but is still continuing today (often with expressions of time such as *always, all week, for* and *since* etc.).	
Have you ever been to Hawaii? Have my tickets to the festival arrived yet? I've reminded you a hundred times about the concert!	in questions and statements about whether something has taken place (often with expressions of time such *as ever, yet, never, twice* etc.).	
Your friend has just phoned. I'm afraid the café has just closed. I've lost my surfboard.	to stress the result of a past activity on the present (often together with *just, this very moment*).	

IF/WHEN + FIRST CONDITIONAL

	Use the first conditional …	Your examples
If the weather's nice, we'll have a picnic.	to talk about probable future consequences. The structure is: *If/when + simple present, will-future*	
We'll watch the match on TV if we can't get tickets.	The *if/when* clause can also follow the consequence.	

THE FUTURE

The main forms to talk about the future are the *will-future* and the *going-to-future*. But it is also possible to use present tenses to talk about the future!

WILL-FUTURE

	Use the will-future …	Your examples
It'll probably rain later. There will be a footpath to the top of the hill.	for predictions or for something you think is (very) likely to happen.	
I think I'll come to the BBQ with you. I'll take some photos, for sure.	for spontaneous decisions and promises.	

GOING-TO-FUTURE

	Use the going-to-future …	Your examples
I'm going to go to the Highlands. Alice is going to sail around the world one day.	for plans and intentions.	

PRESENT CONTINUOUS

	Use the present continuous …	Your examples
My host family is taking me to Dublin on Saturday. We're meeting up later.	for definite arrangements.	

PRESENT SIMPLE

	Use the present simple …	Your examples
The festival starts on Thursday.	for timetable information.	

LANGUAGE SUPPORT

ADJECTIVES: COMPARISON

ADJECTIVE	COMPARATIVE	SUPERLATIVE	Your examples
Many short adjectives add –er or –est.			
high	higher	highest	
strong	stronger	strongest	
Adjectives which already end in –e add –r or –est.			
large	larger	largest	
nice	nicer	nicest	
Short adjectives which end with a consonant double it.			
big	bigger	biggest	
hot	hotter	hottest	
Adjectives which end with –y change this to –ier or –iest.			
cloudy	cloudier	cloudiest	
Adjectives with three or more syllables add more or most.			
beautiful	more beautiful	most beautiful	
exciting	more exciting	most exciting	
Some adjectives are irregular.			
good	better	best	
bad	worse	worst	

ASKING QUESTIONS

		Your examples
Where can you play cricket? What is a regatta? Who wants to come to the fair with me?	**Wh-questions** begin with a wh-word (*what, who, where, when, which, why*) or *how* and ask for information.	
Do you watch 'Stranger Things'? Have you ever played rugby?	**Yes / no questions** begin with an auxiliary verb (*do, be, have*).	

COUNTABLE AND UNCOUNTABLE NOUNS

		Your examples
one hill, a hill, three hills one surfboard, a surfboard, some surfboards	**Countable nouns** are things which can be counted. They have a singular and a plural form. You can use numbers and *a/an/some* with them.	
some jam some information some art	**Uncountable nouns** do not have a plural form. You cannot use numbers or *a/an* with them.	
a jar of jam a piece of information a work of art	Often you can use a quantity word with uncountable nouns.	

FUNCTIONAL REFERENCE

You can find more functional language on pages 4, 10, 16 and 23 of this module and also on the Language Workout pages.

Make a note of any other relevant phrases you hear or come across and add them below.

TALKING ABOUT LIKES, DISLIKES AND PREFERENCES

likes	Your examples
I like … (best / the most / the least).	
I love …	
I enjoy …	
Do you fancy (a coffee / …)?	
My favourite (food / place / …) is …	
I'm keen on …	
… is awesome / cool / great / amazing!	
dislikes	
I don't like …	
I'm not a fan of …	
I'm not keen on …	
I really hate …	
I can't stand …	
… is awful / horrible / disgusting / gross!	
preferences	
You can use *a verb + noun, verb + to infinitive* or *verb + -ing* form	
I prefer black coffee.	
I prefer to drink coffee.	
I prefer swimming (to cycling).	
Do you like dark chocolate? – It's okay, but I prefer milk chocolate.	

LANGUAGE SUPPORT

MAKING REQUESTS

Notice the difference: *I like* = shows preference *I'd like (I would like)* = for requests **You can use *I'd like + noun* or *I'd like + to infinitive***	**Your examples**
What would you like? – I'd like a coffee and a slice of carrot cake, please.	
Could I have some …?	
I'll have today's special, please.	
Would you like some cream with that? – Yes, please. / No, thanks.	
I'd like to go / do / have …	
… and if you're being polite …	
Excuse me, …	
Could I possibly have …?	
I wonder if you could …?	

MAKING SUGGESTIONS AND GIVING ADVICE

	Your examples
Let's …	
How about the blue one?	
How about joining a club?	
Why don't you …?	
We should meet up soon!	
I can recommend …	
You ought to …	
Take your litter with you!	

EXPRESSING ABILITY

	Your examples
She's good at football / keeping secrets.	
I can cook really well.	
I dance really badly.	
Mum can't cook at all, but Dad's a great cook.	

TALKING ABOUT OPINIONS

Stating an opinion	Your examples
I think / believe …	
I am certain / sure that …	
My opinion / view is that …	
I share / don't share your opinion.	
Personally, I think that …	
In my opinion, a vegetarian diet is healthier.	
What's your opinion on this?	
What do you think about / of …?	
How do you feel about that?	
Agreeing	
I totally agree.	
I think you're absolutely right.	
Absolutely!	
Agreed! Cycling is awesome.	
I agree with you 100 %.	
That's so true.	
Disagreeing	
I disagree completely.	
I'm afraid I disagree.	
I don't agree with you.	
Sorry, I think you're wrong. Surfing is much more fun!	
I don't think so.	
No way! *(informal)*	

DESCRIBING PEOPLE, PLACES AND THINGS

	Your examples
It looks / sounds / seems awesome.	
He sounds just like his dad.	
What does it taste like? – It tastes delicious / disgusting / salty / …	
I'm allergic to …	
You're amazing / beautiful!	
It's similar to / identical to …	
He's different from / to his brother.	
The blue shoes are nice. But not as nice as the red ones. And they're nicest in pink!	
Tell me about …	
What's it like?	

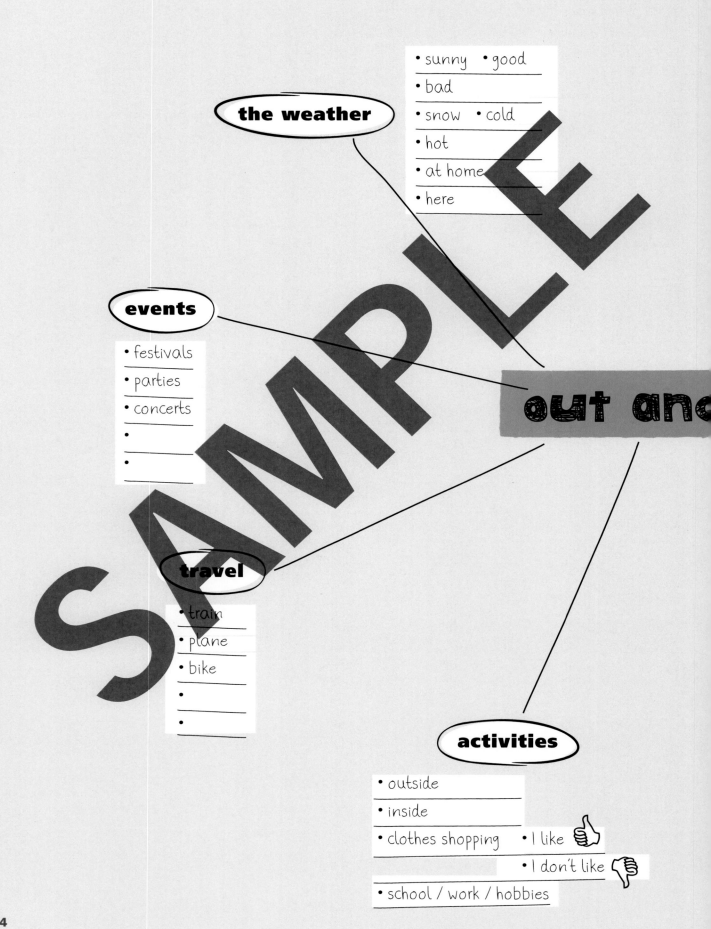

the weather
- sunny • good
- bad
- snow • cold
- hot
- at home
- here

events
- festivals
- parties
- concerts
-
-

SAMPLE

out and

travel
- train
- plane
- bike
-
-

activities
- outside
- inside
- clothes shopping • I like 👍
- I don't like 👎
- school / work / hobbies

Build your own vocabulary mind map!
Add any new words you see or hear.

going on a trip
- packing
  - clothes
  - hiking boots
  - weather protection
  - sunglasses
  - things to do
  - board games
  - useful things
  - map
  - anything else?
- things I want to see and do
- food and refreshments

about

places
- town
- countryside
- seaside
- attractions
- buildings

experiences
- good
- bad
- what I learnt

the weekend
- routine
- things I have to do
- things I want do do
  - my homework
  - clean my room

Words from the week.
Think about the week and add words that will help you talk about your time here.

the project
- topic
- team
- planning
- gathering information
- the result

the experience
- food
- things I tried   • drink
- activities
- things I liked
- things I didn't like so muc

my week here

the trips
- what I saw
- what I learnt
- where to go next time

the people
- where I'm staying
- at the school   • classmates
- the teacher(s
- outside school

the place
- the city / town / village
- the buildings
- where I stayed

what I learnt
- language
- culture
- working together